Christian Krogmann

Tough Economic Climate

What do you think should be Global Purchasing's added contribution in the likely difficult economic climate for business in 2012?

GRIN Publishing

Bibliographic information published by the German National Library:

The German National Library lists this publication in the National Bibliography; detailed bibliographic data are available on the Internet at http://dnb.dnb.de .

Imprint:

Copyright © 2011 GRIN Verlag, Open Publishing GmbH
Print and binding: Books on Demand GmbH, Norderstedt Germany
ISBN: 978-3-656-21084-9

This book at GRIN:

http://www.grin.com/en/e-book/195083/tough-economic-climate

GRIN - Your knowledge has value

Since its foundation in 1998, GRIN has specialized in publishing academic texts by students, college teachers and other academics as e-book and printed book. The website www.grin.com is an ideal platform for presenting term papers, final papers, scientific essays, dissertations and specialist books.

Visit us on the internet:

http://www.grin.com/

http://www.facebook.com/grincom

http://www.twitter.com/grin_com

Heriot-Watt University

School of Management and Languages

MSc Logistics and Supply Chain Management

TOUGH ECONOMIC CLIMATE

What do you think should be Global Purchasing's added contribution in the likely difficult economic climate for business in 2012?

Module Title: Global Purchasing and Supply

Module Code: C11GB

Word Count: 2440 (main text, excl. references)

TABLE OF CONTENTS

LIST OF FIGURES II

1 INTRODUCTION 1

2 CHARACTERISTICS AND PROSPECTS OF THE ECONOMIC CLIMATE 1

3 GLOBAL PURCHASING AND ITS ECONOMIC CONTRIBUTION 5

    3.1   Display of different approaches applicable 5

    3.2   Risk management 6

    3.3   Saving of costs 7

4 CONCLUSION 8

LIST OF REFERENCES 9

LIST OF FIGURES

Figure 1: Real GDP growth..2

Figure 2: Country debts and budget deficits compared..3

Figure 3: World commodity prices, 2000 – 2011 4

Figure 4: Inflation rates per region and year..4

1 INTRODUCTION

Businesses aim to maximise their profits since the beginning of economic thinking. Hence, maximum efficiency and minimum costs play a key role within this thinking (Mankiw, 2011). In this context, purchasing gained much attention in terms of increasingly tough competition as the costs for purchased goods and services add up to around 50 per cent of the total costs for goods sold (COGS) on average (van Weele, 2010). This high proportion illustrates that purchasing encompasses more than the operational buying process. In fact, it is a function that comprises various activities. Van Weele (2010, p.8) defines purchasing as 'the management of the company's external resources in such a way that the supply of all goods, services, capabilities and knowledge which are necessary for running, maintaining and managing the company's primary and support activities is secured at the most favourable conditions'. Consequently, all activities to manage the company's external resources are included in purchasing functions. In recent years it seems this management has become more difficult due to circumstances such as economic, financial and political crises. Even acts of God can lead to greater volatility and uncertainty that may impact the process of purchasing. Hence, in order to cope with the likely tough economic climate in 2012, businesses have to reflect possible strategies. Moreover, due to the increased importance of purchasing and supply management, risks as well as challenges related to these functions have to be pointed out in order to evaluate its contribution for managing the economic situation.

2 CHARACTERISTICS AND PROSPECTS OF THE ECONOMIC CLIMATE

As already mentioned in the assignment's title, businesses likely have to face a tough economic climate in the near future. However, what circumstances represent a tough economic climate? In order to make adequate appraisals regarding the economic activity, experts usually make use of diverse indicators. One of the most common and also most important indicators for the economic activity is the gross domestic product (GDP) (Baumohl, 2008). As it shows how fast or slow an economy grows or shrinks respectively, many economic decisions and forecasts are based on this indicator. With regard to the upcoming year, many different economic research institutes and others such as the International Monetary Fund (IMF) or the World Bank give their predictions concerning the future development of the economic activity. An overview of predicted economic growth is given by

the following figure adapted from the data of the latest world economic outlook of the
International Monetary Fund (2011 b):

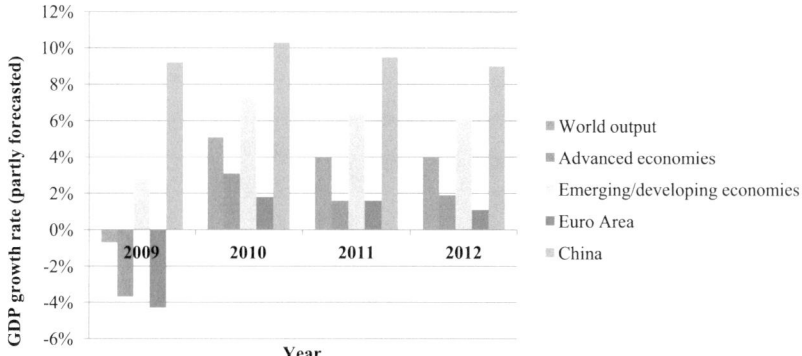

Figure 1: Real GDP growth; Source: International Monetary Fund (2011)

Figure 1 illustrates that the development of GDP growth in advanced economies and
particularly in the Euro Area is fairly different from that of emerging or developing
economies. According to the International Monetary Fund (2011 b) countries such as the
United States, Japan, United Kingdom and also several states of the Euro Area such as
Germany or France are counted among the advanced economies. In contrast, emerging or
developing economies include the BRIC states (Brazil, Russia, India and China) and others.
The IMF forecasts a growth rate of 1.9 % and 6.1 % for advanced economies and emerging
economies respectively in 2012. Furthermore, in comparison to IMF's previous world
economic outlook (International Monetary Fund, 2011 a), the figures were invariably adjusted
downwards. Hence, the economic activity in most of the mentioned economies is predicted to
downgrade. According to this institution, this results from mainly two reasons. Firstly, the
economic recovery in advanced economies is very slow. Secondly, these economies have to
deal with financial problems due to very high debts partly resulting from the economic crisis.

According to the International Monetary Fund (2011 b), the reasons for slowing global
activity are various. In Japan, for instance, the devastating tsunami was responsible for
shrinkage of 0.5 percent of the GDP. Furthermore, the political unrests in countries of the
Middle East and North Africa also had an impact on the global economy, due to sharply
increased oil prices. In addition, the current debt and banking sector problems in the Euro

Area are one further important aspect that needs to be added. Figure 2 illustrates the seriousness of the debt crisis going on in Europe:

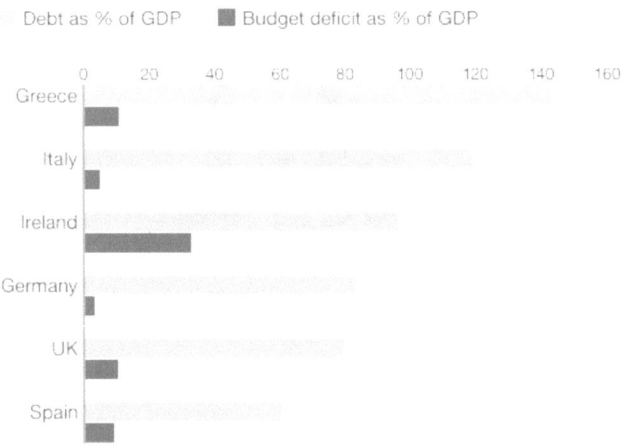

Debt as % of GDP   Budget deficit as % of GDP

Figure 2: Country debts and budget deficits compared; Source: BBC (2011 a)

To illustrate this point one need only refer to the current situation in Greece. In order to prevent the state from bankruptcy rigorous fiscal consolidation is needed and other European partners are forced to support with financial guarantees regulated in the European Financial Stability Facility (EFSF, 2011). These financial problems that also occur in other European states are responsible for a predicted shrinkage of the GDP within the Euro Area in 2012. Besides the Euro Area, the United States still faces problems regarding its economic activity. According to the International Monetary Fund (2011 b) the shift from public to private demand takes more time than expected. A major reason for this is the high unemployment rate. To counter this development, a job creation initiative of $ 447 billion is planned (BBC, 2011 b). The last few days gave an idea of slight recovery, as the GDP growth rate of the last quarter doubled in comparison to the former one (U.S. Department of Commerce, 2011). Nevertheless, the International Monetary Fund (2011 b) considers future development to be fairly risky. This results mainly from uncertainty and fallen confidence. This fallen confidence in the markets is represented by the different stock indices which also fell sharply due to the news regarding debt crisis and other economic impacts (CNN Money, 2011; Kollewe and Treanor, 2011).

Not only slow economic growth but also other important aspects need to be mentioned with respect to a tough economic climate for businesses in 2012. Due to the financial problems, bank lending is fairly tight. Small and medium sized enterprises (SMEs), in particular, are forced to delay their investments as they have difficulties to get corresponding loans (Clifford, 2011). In addition to these difficulties, businesses are confronted with increasing commodity prices. Figure 3 illustrates the corresponding development:

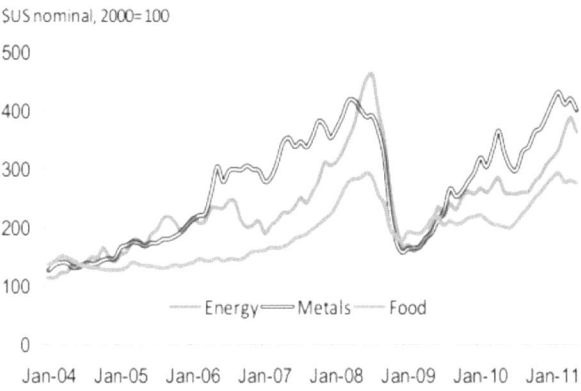

Figure 3: World commodity prices, 2000 – 2011; Source: The World Bank (2011)

Doubtless, an increase in the mentioned commodity prices gets observable when examining the graph. These high prices mainly result from strong economic growth in emerging and developing economies. According to the World Bank (2011) the high commodity prices are a driver for accelerated inflation. This can be proved by the following figure:

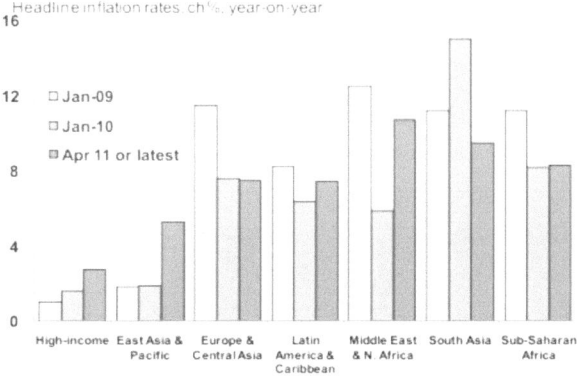

Figure 4: Inflation rates per region and year; Source: The World Bank (2011)

Figure 4 illustrates the increasing inflation in different economies. Compared with the aims of the European Central Bank, for instance, which targets a maximum inflation rate of 2 percent (European Central Bank, n.d.), the illustrated inflation rates are fairly high.

From these exemplified developments one must conclude that the economic climate is indeed going to be tough in the near future. Nevertheless, it has to be evaluated to what extent these developments can be countered or at least handled by a business and in particular by its purchasing function. This evaluation will be made in the following chapter.

3 GLOBAL PURCHASING AND ITS ECONOMIC CONTRIBUTION

As already mentioned in the introduction, purchasing is increasingly constituted as one of the key drivers for successful business (van Weele, 2010). Especially in critical situations, businesses are able to reduce costs quickly with help of their purchasing function (Bogaschewsky and Müller, n.d.). On the other hand, Bogaschewsky and Müller (n.d.) argue that companies must not only focus on short term cost reductions but they also have to think in the long term. This conforms to the statement that purchasing has developed from an operational to a strategically important function (Humphreys, McIvor and McAleer, 2000). In further literature it is pointed out that purchasing also has to deal with risk management, particularly in tough economic times (Schuh et al., 2011). Furthermore, Bogaschewsky and Müller (n.d.) state that companies have to be aware of the importance of each of the company's suppliers. The last two statements identify supply risk and supplier importance as dependent variables regarding a corresponding strategy.

3.1 Display of different approaches applicable

From the previously mentioned arguments one must conclude that there is no all-embracing business strategy as there are at least two variables that should be considered. Supply risk and supplier importance, i.e. profit or financial impact are also the main criteria in Kraljic's purchasing portfolio (van Weele, 2010). In this approach, the profit impact includes criteria such as purchasing costs, costs of materials, purchased volume or impact on business growth. In contrast, the supply risk comprises criteria such as product availability, number of suppliers available, inventory risks or available substitutes (van Weele, 2010). With the aid of these criteria, suppliers or products can be categorized in four different classes: leverage (high financial impact, low supply risk), routine (low financial impact and low supply risk), bottleneck (low financial impact, high supply risk) and strategic (high financial impact, high supply risk). As previously mentioned, it is necessary to distinguish between these different categories in order to determine the corresponding strategies. According to Kraljic cited in van Weele (2010) the relative strength should be for the benefit of the buyer in order to avoid noticeable dependence on the company's suppliers. Nevertheless, the classification of suppliers and products in this case is to be understood in a general view.

3.2 Risk management

Hence, what strategies have to be applied in tough economic situations such as the current one? The role of supplier selection and an appropriate risk management are major tasks of purchasing (Ravindran et al., 2010) and also Schuh et al. (2011) set priority to risk management. Being also important in general, it gains in importance particularly in tough economic times as each company can indirectly be struck by ups and downs in the market via its suppliers. This applies particularly to small suppliers that could, for instance, face a dilemma regarding their creditworthiness due to tight bank lending. Hence, in order to ensure continuous performance, the company should conduct an appropriate risk management (Schuh et al., 2011). Correspondingly, the higher the supply risks, the greater the need for action, i.e. risk management is important for bottleneck and strategic products or suppliers in particular. According to Schuh et al. (2011), an adequate risk management comprises mainly 3 steps:

- The identification of risky suppliers or products, i.e. the analysis of those which, for instance, have poor availability or its substitutes are limited
- The definition of strategies, i.e. the consideration of actions that must be taken to cope with the risks
- The implementation of the strategies in the daily business, i.e. continuous reporting and analysis of the supplier performance in order to detect occurring problems as early as possible

Depending on the importance of the product or supplier, Schuh et al. (2011) propose different strategies. Those with high importance, i.e. high financial impact, must be handled most accurately. Schuh et al. (2011) and also Bogaschewsky and Müller (n.d.) state that these suppliers and their supplied products must be obligated to the company by intensifying the collaboration. Thus, the suppliers are made more dependent on the company. Furthermore, by applying collaborative actions such as planning or forecasting, the supply risks can be reduced (Danese, 2007). It is clear that these actions are also useful for sustainable success and not only for managing a tough economic climate. Bogaschewsky and Müller (n.d.) go further by stating that in case of crucial supplier relationships the corresponding risk management has to include also other participating parties such as 2nd and 3rd tier suppliers etc. in order to cope with these risks.

On the other hand, Schuh et al. (2011) suggest to get rid of suppliers or products with high supply risk but only low financial impact in case there are opportunities to change these. At this juncture, knowing an adequate substitute is absolutely necessary. If there is no possibility to change, Schuh et al. (2011) suggest supporting the suppliers, e.g. by reducing the due date for payment in order to improve their situation and hence minimise the potential risks. Suppliers or products with low supply risk and financial impact should be observed continuously in order to discover potential problems timely.

3.3 Saving of costs

Besides risk management it might nevertheless be necessary to reduce costs in order to stay competitive, especially in a polypolistic market structure, where prices have to be considered as fixed (Bogaschewsky and Müller, n.d.). Within these markets, a company is not able to raise prices at random as buyers would in this case substitute the vendor. Schuh et al. (2011) propose four different strategies to reduce costs depending on the situation of supply and demand:

A purchasing company with a high buyer power should be able to reduce costs easily, because its supplier base for single products – provided that it is polypolistic – is very dependent on the company's orders. Hence, the purchasing company can achieve lower purchasing prices by using techniques such as tenders. In case the company has strategic suppliers that are comparably powerful, Schuh et al. (2011) suggest focusing on the long term collaboration instead of a downward pressure on the prices. In order to reduce costs in this case, the collaboration should include classic supply chain improvement tools and techniques such as lean management (Christopher, 2011).

In contrast, purchasing companies with only low buyer power and corresponding suppliers with high selling power do not have good opportunities to bargain prices. Instead, they should try to analyse the root causes for the dependence and focus on basic changes in order to shift the balance of power (Schuh et al., 2011). Lastly, in case of low buying and selling power – which is the case when the company purchases or the supplier sells goods or services not necessarily required – the purchasing company should tie the requirements and hence try to bargain discounts. Furthermore, it has to analyze whether the goods or services are inevitable (Schuh et al., 2011).

4   CONCLUSION

Businesses have to face a tough economic climate in the near future. This assumption can undoubtedly be approved by analyzing different indicators provided by different institutions. In this context, the major statement is uncertainty as there are different developments in different regions that all might influence the global economic activity. Continuous growth in emerging and developing economies and contrary developments in advanced economies which have to struggle with debts make the markets fairly uncertain. The preceding paragraphs gave an idea about the question how companies can cope with the tough economic climate and what purchasing's added contribution might be. The first idea is always to cut costs. Although it might be necessary, businesses also have to keep thinking in the long term. Therefore, cost savings should not primarily be made by reducing prices but by trying to improve processes and build up collaborations. The supply risk and corresponding risk management should play a key role within this thinking as it enables the company to both reduce costs and improve processes at the same time. Single actions such as sourcing strategies each can be seen as possibilities. However, all these thoughts are usually included in those of costs savings and risk management. Hence, these two approaches have to be seen as more general strategies for companies to cope with a tough economic climate.

LIST OF REFERENCES

Baumohl, B. (2008) *The secrets of economic indicators. Hidden clues to future economic trends and investment opportunities*, 2nd edition, Upper Saddle River, N.J: Wharton School Pub.

BBC (2011 a) *Factors behind market turmoil* [online], 27 Oct, Available from: http://www.bbc.co.uk/news/business-14418539 (Accessed 13 Nov 2011).

BBC (2011 b) *Obama lays down gauntlet to Senate on American Jobs Act* [online], 06 Oct, Available from: http://www.bbc.co.uk/news/world-us-canada-15203542 (Accessed 12 Nov 2011).

Bogaschewsky, R. and Müller, H. *Global sourcing portal* [online], Available from: http://www.supply-markets.com/Marktwahl/Downloads/Einkauf_in_der_Krise_WWW.pdf (Accessed 13 Nov 2011).

Christopher, M. (2011) *Logistics & supply chain management*, 4th edition, Harlow: Pearson.

Clifford, C. (2011) 'Small business lending plummets', *CNN Money* [online], 16 Jun, Available from: http://money.cnn.com/2011/06/16/smallbusiness/small_business_lending/index.htm (Accessed 13 Nov 2011).

CNN Money (2011) *World markets* [online], 13 Nov, Available from: http://money.cnn.com/data/world_markets/europe/ (Accessed 13 Nov 2011).

Danese, P. (2007) 'Designing CPFR collaborations: insights from seven case studies', *International Journal of Operations & Production Management*, pp. 181-204.

EFSF (2011) *European Financial Stability Facility* [online], Available from: http://www.efsf.europa.eu/about/index.htm (Accessed 08 Nov 2011).

European Central Bank *The ECB's monetary policy strategy* [online], Available from: http://www.ecb.eu/mopo/intro/html/index.en.html (Accessed 13 Nov 2011).

Humphreys, P., McIvor, R. and McAleer, E. (2000) 'Re-engineering the purchasing function', *European Journal of Purchasing & Supply Management*, no. 6/2000, pp. 85-93.

International Monetary Fund (2011 a) *World economic outlook April 2011. Tensions from the two-speed recovery. Unemployment, commodities, and capital flows*, Washington, D.C.: International Monetary Fund.

International Monetary Fund (2011 b) *World economic outlook September 2011. Slowing growth, rising risks*, Washington, D.C.: International Monetary Fund.

Kollewe, J. and Treanor, J. (2011) 'Debt crisis: stock markets panic', *The Guardian* [weblog], 5 Aug, Available from: http://www.guardian.co.uk/business/blog/2011/aug/05/stock-market-crisis-ftse-usa-europe (Accessed 13 Nov 2011).

Mankiw, N.G. (2011) *Principles of economics*, 6th edition, Mason: South-Western Cengage Learning.

Ravindran, A.R., Bilsel, R.U., Wadhwa, V. and Yang, T. (2010) 'Risk adjusted multicriteria supplier selection models with applications', *International Journal of Production Research*, 15 Jan, pp. 405-424.

Schuh, C., Kromoser, R., Strohmer, M.F., Pérez, R.R. and Triplat, A. (2011) *Der agile Einkauf*, Wiesbaden: Gabler.

The World Bank (2011) *Global economic prospects* [online], Jun, Available from: http://siteresources.worldbank.org/INTGEP/Resources/335315-1307471336123/7983902-1307479336019/Full-Report.pdf (Accessed 13 Nov 2011).

U.S. Department of Commerce (2011) *U.S. Economy at a Glance: Perspective from the BEA Accounts* [online], 27 Oct, Available from: http://www.bea.gov/newsreleases/glance.htm (Accessed 12 Nov 2011).

van Weele, A.J. (2010) *Purchasing & supply chain management. Analysis, strategy, planning and practice*, 5th edition, Andover: Cengage Learning.